tiger

Jinny Johnson

MARSHALL PUBLISHING • LONDON

Moti was born in a dark cave. At first he stayed close to his mother and drank her milk. Now he is ready to explore the world outside.

Tiger cubs love to play. Look at Moti attacking the leaves. This is a good way for him to practise his hunting skills.

Moti notices any little movements in the grass. Tigers have very sharp eyes and good hearing.

In the middle
of the day it is
too hot to play.
Moti sleeps.

Tigers like water and often enjoy a cooling swim. But they hate getting their faces wet.

Moti's mother will teach him how to catch other animals to eat. Look at his big paws and sharp teeth.

Moti's stripy coat hides him in the long grass. He is off to have his first lesson in hunting. Good luck, Moti.